CONTENTS

GW00730495

CURRICULUM LINKS

SONG 1   BOO HOO!

Science: Talk about babies and what they need to keep healthy and happy, eg food, water, sleep etc. Discuss what could be making baby Jesus cry? Does he need food, or perhaps just a cuddle?

History: Do the children know anyone who's just had a baby? Was the baby born at home or in a hospital? Talk about how there wouldn't have been hospitals the way we have them today, when Jesus was born. Can the children think of anything else that might be different about having babies now rather than 2000 years ago? (Eg nappies, clothes, pushchairs etc.)

SONG 2   I HAVE A LITTLE PRESENT

Creative development: With the children, design and make some wrapping paper and use it to wrap presents for under the Christmas tree.

SONG 3   EMERALD

Design and technology / Creative development:
Design and make a crown using card, paints, glitter and some 'emeralds'!

History: Look at some pictures of kings and queens from biblical times to the present day. Look at the sorts of clothes they wore. Did they wear crowns with precious stones?

SONG 4   ENORMOUS ELEPHANTS

Physical development: Along with the music, pretend to be a herd of heavy-footed elephants. Move slowly, then faster. Perhaps have a leader and follow on, one behind the other.

SONG 5	A GRAND SONG

Music

Sing this song in a shy and timid way. Ask the children if they think this sounds like a 'grand choir'. Now try singing it in a bold, confident way. Which way do the children think suits the song best?

Explore expression through music by singing other songs in different ways, eg sing *Twinkle, Twinkle Little Star,* very fast, then very loud, then in a sad way, then in a happy way. Which way do the children think best suits the song?

SONG 6	DANCING SONG

Creative development and *Physical development:*

This song is ideal for music and movement. Practise and perform the actions that the song suggests - using the instrumental section of the song to really show off your moves!

SONG 8	JUST A KISS

Communication, language & literacy:

Have a group discussion about what the children think could be more important – having lots of nice things or being kind, thoughtful and loving towards each other.

Personal, social and emotional development:

Can they think of anything kind that someone has done for them recently? (Eg shared something, gave them a hug.) How did it make them feel? Have they done something thoughtful for someone else?

SONG 9	A GIFT FOR THE BABY BOY

Geography:

In this song, we're all going on a journey to Bethlehem. Look at where the children live on a globe, and then look to see where Bethlehem is on the globe.

Do any of the children have a friend or relation who lives in a different country? Talk about the name of the country and try and find it on the globe.

CHARACTER LIST

Narrator Can be read by an adult/older child, or split between a group of pupils.

Boy A leading roll with an important final scene! (A girl could just as well play this role – with the tiniest bit of script editing.)

Messenger Another key role, ideal for a confident budding actor/ess.

Prince A small part with just one line.

Queen Another small part with just one line.

Nobleman And again, a small part with just one line!

King With authority, and just one line to remember.

Pharaoh You've guessed it – one more line, delivered with stature!

Elephants Non-speaking parts to help act out Song 4. Use as many as you like and adapt the song to fit.

Choir You may choose to use all the children for this, or select just a few to be the 'mighty choir' in Song 5.

Dancers Graceful little cherubs to dance in Song 6. No speaking lines to learn.

Stable characters You may want to have a stable scene on stage, with Mary, Joseph and the baby Jesus. All non-speaking parts – except for the baby's cries!

STAGING & PROPS

The staging is entirely up to you here. You'll need to consider having a stable scene on stage, as most of the characters will visit the baby Jesus with their gifts. Using a 'crying' baby doll for Jesus would be good. Another idea would be to have all the characters around the edge of the stage, stepping forward when it's their turn to perform.

SCRIPT AND SONG LYRICS

NARRATOR: A long time ago, a lady called Mary and a man called Joseph went to Bethlehem. They stayed in a little stable and in that stable a very special baby was born. He was called Jesus.

Mary and Joseph were very happy to have their new baby, but Jesus wasn't happy at all. He cried and cried and cried and cried. Nobody could make him happy and nobody knew what to do.

Song 1. BOO HOO!

1 Boo hoo, boo hoo, we don't know what to do,
The baby's been crying all night.
Boo hoo, boo hoo, we don't know what to do,
Nothing we do is right.

2 Boo hoo, boo hoo, we don't know what to do,
The baby's been crying all night.
Boo hoo, boo hoo, we don't know what to do,
Nothing we do is right.
Please stop crying, baby Jesus,
We don't know what to do.

3 *Repeat verse 2*

4 Boo hoo, boo hoo, we don't know what to do,
The baby's been crying all night.
Boo hoo, boo hoo, we don't know what to do,
Nothing we do is, nothing we do is,
Nothing we do is right!

© 2003 Out of the Ark Music, Surrey KT12 4RQ

NARRATOR: A messenger went out to see if he could find anyone who could stop the baby Jesus crying. The messenger found a little boy.

BOY: I know what to do. The baby Jesus needs a present.

MESSENGER: Good idea. I'll find somebody rich who can give him a really good present!

BOY: I can give him a present!

Song 2. I HAVE A LITTLE PRESENT

1 I have a little present,
It didn't cost a lot,
I have a little present,
It's all I've got.

2 It's just a little something,
It didn't cost a lot,
It's just a little something,
It's all I've got.

Instrumental

3 I have a little present,
It didn't cost a lot,
I have a little present,
It's all I've got.

BOY: I can give him a present!

MESSENGER: But you are just a little boy and a little present is no good!

NARRATOR: The messenger went and found a tall prince, a fine queen and a great nobleman.

PRINCE: I will give the baby an enormous emerald!

QUEEN: I will give the baby a silver ring!

NOBLEMAN: I will give the baby an enormous diamond!

Song 3. EMERALD

1   Look at the emerald glowing green,
Shiny in my hand,
Look at the emerald glowing green,
Shiny in my hand,
Fit for a king,
Great wealth to bring.

2   Look at the silver ring, fine and new,
Shiny in my hand,
Look at the silver ring, fine and new,
Shiny in my hand,
Fit for a king,
Great wealth to bring.

3   Look at the diamond, sparkling bright,
Shiny in my hand,
Look at the diamond, sparkling bright,
Shiny in my hand,
Fit for a king,
Great wealth to bring.

NARRATOR: The prince, the queen and the nobleman went and gave their gifts to the baby, but the baby kept on crying. He cried and cried and cried and cried! The messenger went and found a great king.

MESSENGER: Can you make the baby Jesus happy?

KING: I will give the baby <u>four</u> enormous elephants!

NARRATOR: The king gathered up the enormous elephants and went to see the baby.

Song 4. ENORMOUS ELEPHANTS

1   One enormous elephant, fit for a king,
Lumbering down to Bethlehem,
One enormous elephant swinging his trunk,
And trumpeting with all his might,
Yes, trumpeting with all his might!

2   Two enormous elephants, fit for a king,
    Lumbering down to Bethlehem,
    Two enormous elephants swinging their trunks,
    And trumpeting with all their might,
    Yes, trumpeting with all their might!

3   Three enormous elephants ...

4   Four enormous elephants ...

> For a bigger production, you might like to count up in 2s, eg:
>
> Two enormous elephants, fit for a king ...
>
> Four enormous elephants, fit for a king ...
>
> Six enormous elephants, fit for a king ...

NARRATOR: The baby saw the elephants, but he kept on crying. He cried and cried and cried and cried. The messenger set out to search again. This time he went to see all the very finest singers in the land. They formed a mighty choir. The choir went to see the baby and they sang for Jesus, a very grand song indeed.

Song 5. A GRAND SONG

1   We are a mighty choir,
    Our voices are very loud,
    And we will sing a song for you,
    With a mighty sound.
    Tra-la-la, tra-la-la,
    A grand song this is,
    Tra-la-la, tra-la-la,
    A grand song this is.

Repeat 2 more times

NARRATOR:	But the baby didn't like the grand song. He still cried and cried and cried and cried! The messenger left the stable. He walked around thinking and thinking and wondering what to do. Then he saw the little boy again.
BOY:	Can I give my present to Jesus?
NARRATOR:	But the messenger shook his head at the boy and walked on. He went to see a great pharaoh.
PHARAOH:	I will send my best dancers to the baby.
NARRATOR:	So the pharaoh's dancers went to the baby and they danced a wonderful dance.

Song 6. DANCING SONG

1   Point our toes, point our toes,
    Stretch our graceful arms,
    Point our toes, point our toes,
    Stretch our graceful arms,
    We can dance, we're dancing for the baby.

2   Tip-toe high, tip-toe high,
    Turn ourselves around,
    Tip-toe high, tip-toe high,
    Turn ourselves around,
    We can dance, we're dancing for the baby.

    Instrumental

3   Lightly jump, lightly jump,
    Keeping to the beat,
    Lightly jump, lightly jump,
    Keeping to the beat,
    We can dance, we're dancing for the baby.
    We can dance, we're dancing for the baby.

NARRATOR:	The dancers danced and danced, but still, the baby cried and cried. The messenger left the stable. He really didn't know what to do next. Then he saw the little boy again.

BOY: Can I give my present to the baby now?

MESSENGER: But you are just a little boy!

BOY: Please!!!

MESSENGER: Oh, go on then!

NARRATOR: The little boy went into the stable.

Song 7. I HAVE A LITTLE PRESENT (Reprise)

1 I have a little present,
   it didn't cost a lot,
   I have a little present,
   It's all I've got.

2 It's just a little something,
   It didn't cost a lot,
   It's just a little something,
   It's all I've got.

NARRATOR: The baby was still crying. Everyone waited to see the present that the little boy had brought. He went up to the manger, he looked at the baby Jesus. He leaned over and do you know what he gave him? He gave the baby a kiss. And guess what? The baby stopped crying!

Song 8. JUST A KISS

1 Just a kiss is all it takes, it's simple,
   Just a kiss is all it takes, it's simple,
   All the presents in the world
   Could never be as good as just a kiss.

2 Just a thought inside your heart, it's simple,
   Just a thought inside your heart, it's simple,
   All the presents in the world
   Could never be as good as just a kiss.

   Repeat verse 1

NARRATOR: The little boy's kiss made everyone realise that it's not the size or cost of a gift that matters – it's the love in our hearts, and how we express it, that makes people happy.

What can you bring as a gift to Jesus this Christmas?

Song 9. A GIFT FOR THE BABY BOY

1   Would you like to see,
A tiny child, a tiny child?
Would you like to see,
A child in Bethlehem?

Can you bring a gift for him,
A gift for him tonight?
Can you bring a gift for him?
A gift for the baby boy.
Can you bring a gift for him,
A gift for him tonight?
Can you bring a gift for him?
A gift for the baby boy.

2   Come down through the streets,
And make your way, and make your way.
Come down through the streets,
And see the baby boy.

Chorus

Boo Hoo!

Words and Music by
Niki Davies

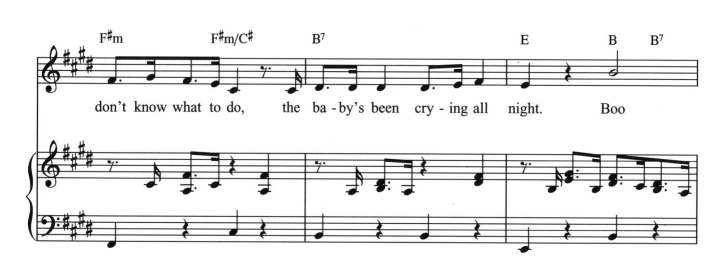

right. Boo right. Please stop cry-ing,

ba-by Je-sus, we don't know what to do. Boo

3rd time D.% al Coda

CODA

no-thing we do is, no-thing we do is,

no-thing we do is right!

13

I Have A Little Present

Words and Music by
Niki Davies

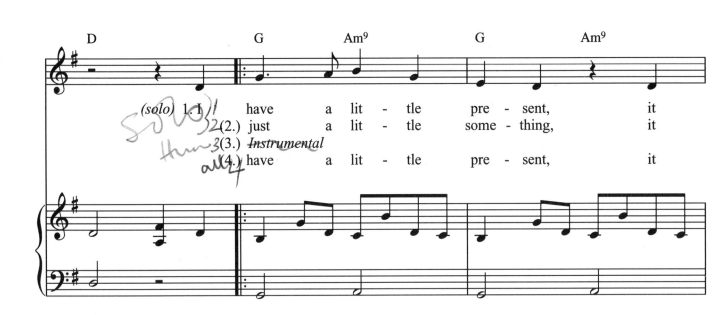

(solo) 1.(1.) I have a lit - tle pre - sent, it
2.(2.) just a lit - tle some - thing, it
3.(3.) *Instrumental*
(4.) have a lit - tle pre - sent, it

did - n't cost a lot.   I   have a lit - tle
did - n't cost a lot.   It's   just a lit - tle
did - n't cost a lot.   I   have a lit - tle

Emerald

Words and Music by
Niki Davies

Steadily (♩ = 122)

1. Look at the e - mer - ald glow - ing green, shi - ny in___ my
2. Look at the sil - ver ring fine and new, shi - ny in___ my
3. Look at the dia - mond spark - ling bright, shi - ny in___ my

Con Pedale

hand. Look at the e - mer - ald glow - ing green,
hand. Look at the sil - ver ring fine and new,
hand. Look at the dia - mond spark - ling bright,

16

Enormous Elephants

Words and Music by
Niki Davies

18

A Grand Song

Words and Music by
Niki Davies

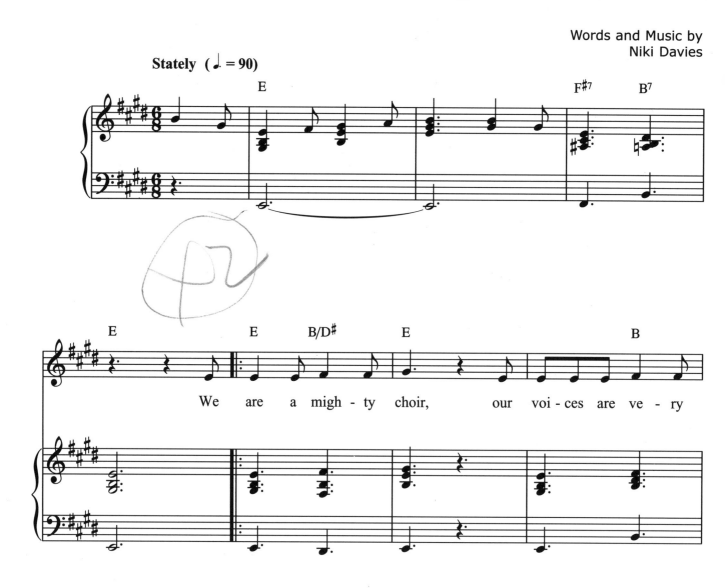

We are a migh-ty choir, our voi-ces are ve-ry

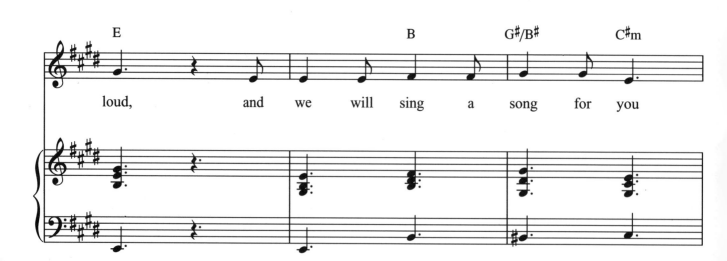

loud, and we will sing a song for you

with a migh-ty sound. Tra-la-la, tra-la-la, a

grand song this is. Tra-la-la, tra-la-la, a

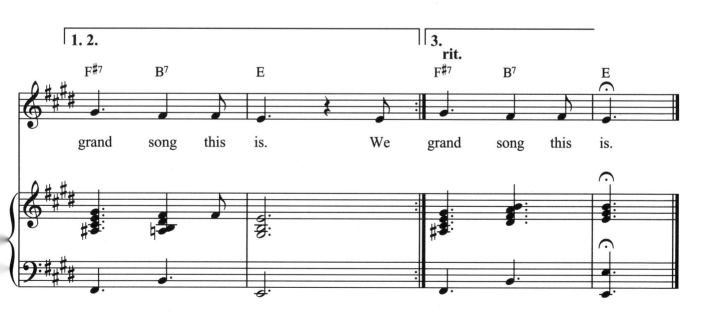

1. 2. grand song this is. We **3.** *rit.* grand song this is.

Dancing Song

Words and Music by
Niki Davies

23

I Have A Little Present

(reprise)

Words and Music by
Niki Davies

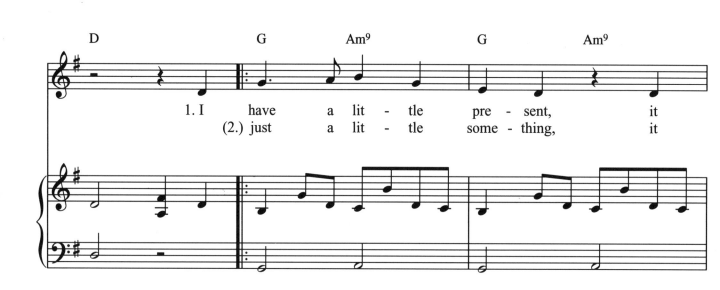

1. I have a lit - tle pre - sent, it
(2.) just a lit - tle some - thing, it

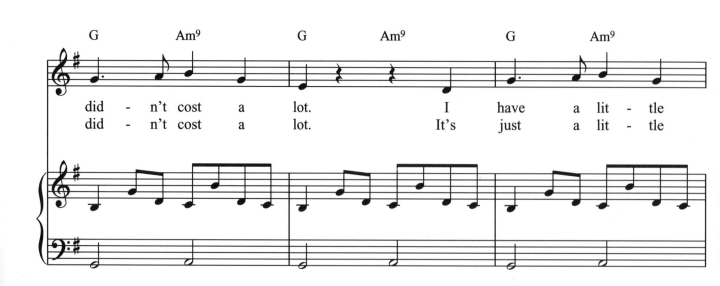

did - n't cost a lot. I have a lit - tle
did - n't cost a lot. It's just a lit - tle

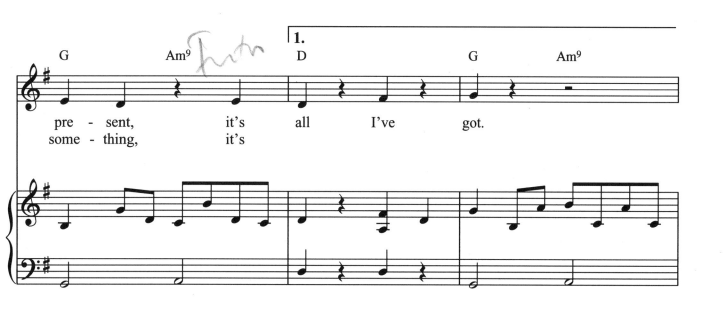

pre - sent, it's all I've got.
some - thing, it's

2. It's

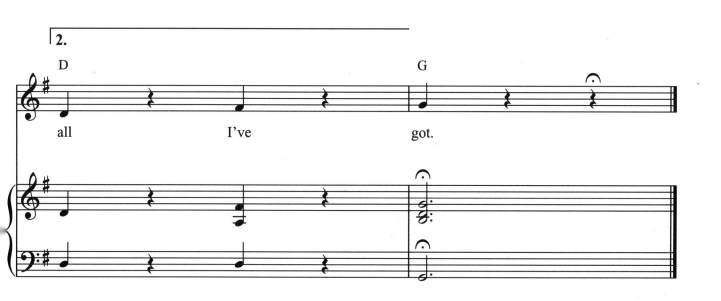

all I've got.

Just A Kiss

Words and Music by
Niki Davies

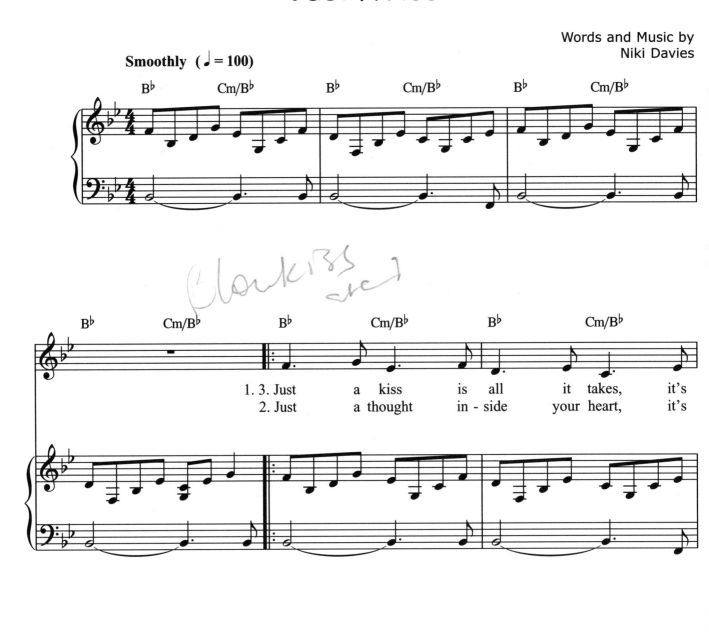

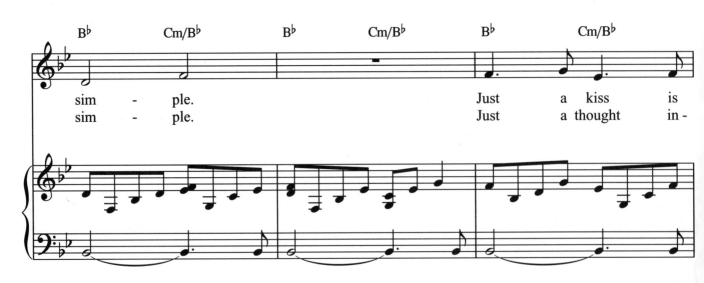

26

all   it   takes,   it's   sim   -   ple.
- side   your   heart,   it's   sim   -   ple.

All   the   pre   -   sents   in   the   world   could
All   the   pre   -   sents   in   the   world   could

1. 2.

ne   -   ver   be   as   good   as   just   a
ne   -   ver   be   as   good   as   just   a

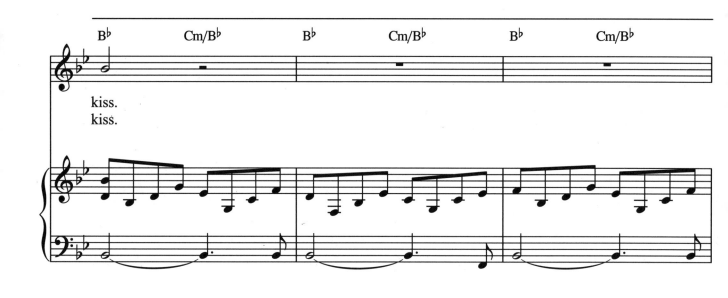

kiss.
kiss.

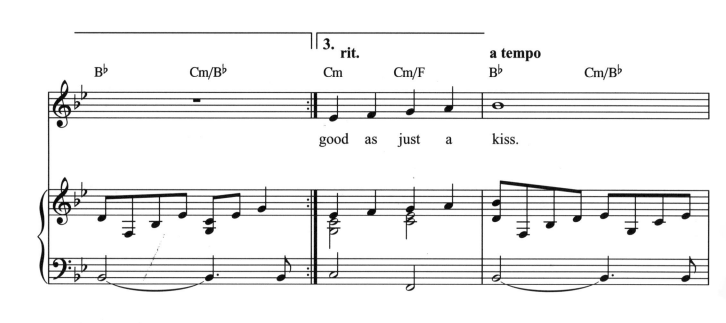

3. *rit.*　　　　*a tempo*

good　as　just　a　kiss.

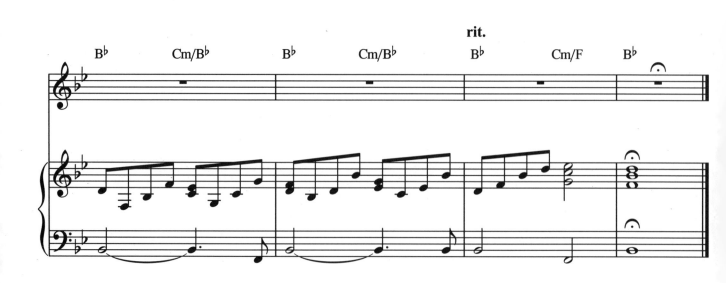

rit.

A Gift For The Baby Boy

Words and Music by
Niki Davies

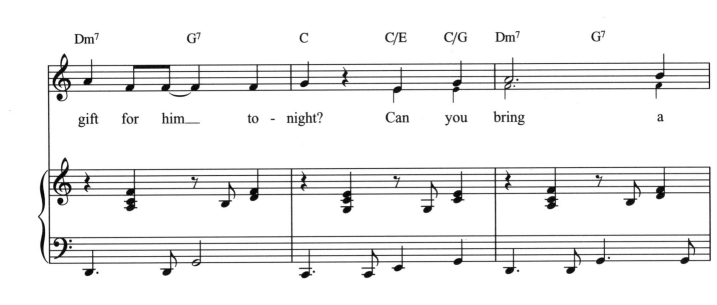

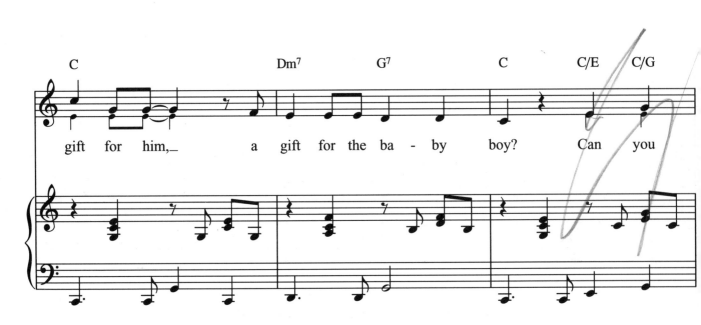

bring a gift for him,__ a gift for him to -

- night? Can you bring a gift for him,__ a

gift for the ba - by boy? boy?

(<u>UK</u> / <u>EIRE</u> / <u>EU</u>)* LICENCE APPLICATION FORM

*To stage this play in <u>non-EU</u> countries please contact Out of the Ark Music for an alternative form.

If you perform A Present For The Baby to an audience other than children and staff you will need to photocopy and complete this form and return it by post or fax to Out of the Ark Music in order to apply for a licence. ***If anticipated audience sizes are very small or if special circumstances apply please contact us.***

We wish to apply for a licence to perform 'A Present For The Baby' by Niki Davies

Customer number (if known): ....

Name of school / organisation: ....

Name of organiser / producer: ....

Date(s) of performance(s): ....

Invoice address: ....
....
....
....

Post code: .... **Country:** ....

Telephone number: ....

Number of performances (excl. dress rehearsal)	**Performances without admission charges**	**Performances with admission charges**
1	☐ £11.75* (inc VAT)	☐ £17.63* (inc VAT)
2	☐ £17.63* (inc VAT)	☐ £23.50* (inc VAT)

Tick one of the boxes above. For 3 or more performances contact Out of the Ark Music for details.

Tick one of the three payment options below: *(Invoices will be sent with all licences)*

☐ Please bill me / my school or nursery at the above address

☐ I enclose a cheque (pounds sterling) for £   payable to **Out of the Ark Music**

☐ Please charge the following card: (VISA, MasterCard and American Express accepted)

Card no:		Expiry date:	_ _ / _ _ (MM/YY)

If the performance is to be recorded in order to sell the recording to parents or to the public please contact Out of the Ark Music. We convey to the licence holder the right to reproduce printed lyrics of the songs in programmes distributed to the audience. The following credit should be included with the lyrics: *'Reproduced by kind permission. © Out of the Ark Music'*

Address: Out of the Ark Music
Sefton House
2 Molesey Road
Hersham Green
Walton-on-Thames
Surrey KT12 4RQ
United Kingdom

Phone: +44 (0)1932 232 250
Fax: +44 (0)1932 703 010
Email: info@outoftheark.com

*The licence fees shown on this form are for 2003–2004 and may be subject to revision.